Step-by-Step Transformations

Turning Beans into Chocolate

Herald McKinley

Cavendish
Square

New York

Published in 2015 by Cavendish Square Publishing, LLC
243 5th Avenue, Suite 136, New York, NY 10016

Library of Congress Cataloging-in-Publication Data
McKinley, Herald.
Turning beans into chocolate / by Herald McKinley.
p. cm. — (Step-by-step transformations)
Includes index.
ISBN 978-1-62713-004-2 (hardcover) ISBN 978-1-62713-005-9 (paperback) ISBN 978-1-62713-006-6 (ebook)
1. Chocolate — Juvenile literature. 2. Cacao — Juvenile literature. 3. Chocolate processing — Juvenile literature. I. McKinley, Herald. II. Title.

TP640.M38 2015
664.5—d23

Editorial Director: Dean Miller
Editor: Amy Hayes
Copy Editor: Cynthia Roby
Art Director: Jeffrey Talbot
Designer: Joseph Macri
Photo Researcher: J8 Media
Production Manager: Jennifer Ryder-Talbot
Production Editor: David McNamara

The photographs in this book are used by permission and through the courtesy of: Cover photo by Food and Drink/SuperStock; © iStockphoto.com/peepo;
Cristian Baitg/E+/Getty Images, 5; © iStockphoto.com/PauloVilela, 7; © iStockphoto.com/joshuaraineyphotography, 9; Kevork Djansezian/Getty Images, 11;
© iStockphoto.com/panchof, 13; Andy Reitz, 15; Gary Ombler/Dorling Kindersley/Getty Images, 17; © Bon Appetit/Alamy, 19;
Ursula Alter/Stockbyte/Getty Images, 21; Back Cover: Visage/Stockbyte/Getty Images.

Printed in the United States of America

Contents

Chocolate is made from cocoa beans.

To make chocolate, first cocoa beans are taken out of a **cocoa pod**.

7

Next, the cocoa beans are left outside on big trays to dry out.

They stay outside for several days.

9

The cocoa beans are cooked.

They become very hot.

11

Then, the cocoa beans are cracked open.

The inside of the bean is called the **nib**.

13

After that, a **machine** grinds the nibs.

The nibs become a **paste**.

15

Next, **cocoa butter** and sugar are added to the paste.

This makes the paste sweet.

Machines mix everything together to make chocolate.

17

After that, the chocolate is put into the last machine.

This machine makes sure the chocolate is the perfect thickness.

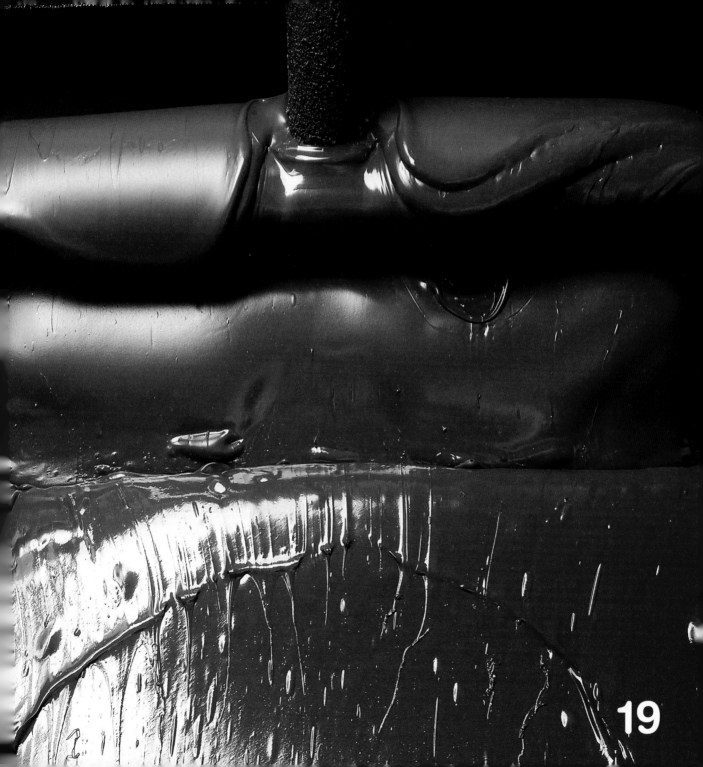

19

Now, the chocolate can be used to make candy.

21

Words to Know

cocoa butter (KO-ko BUH-ter) – a fat-like butter made from cocoa beans

cocoa pod (KO-ko PAHD) – a fruit from the cocoa plant that has beans inside

grind (GRYND) – crushing something into small pieces by putting it into a special machine

machine (muh-SHEEN) – equipment with moving parts that are used to do a job

nib (NIB) – the inside of the cocoa bean

paste (PAYST) – a soft, moist mixture made by grinding food

Find Out More

Books

From Cocoa Bean to Chocolate

Robin Nelson

Lerner Publishing Group

The Story of Chocolate

Russell Punter and Katie Daynes

Usborne Publishing

Website

Hershey's Videos

How We Make Chocolate

www.hersheys.com/ads-and-videos/how-we-make-chocolate.aspx

Index